Original title:
A Song of the Tropics

Copyright © 2025 Creative Arts Management OÜ
All rights reserved.

Author: Nathaniel Blackwood
ISBN HARDBACK: 978-1-80581-621-8
ISBN PAPERBACK: 978-1-80581-148-0
ISBN EBOOK: 978-1-80581-621-8

Portrait of an Island's Pulse

When coconuts start to sway,
The crabs hold a fancy ball,
With little hats and tiny shoes,
They dance until the nightfall.

The sun shines like a big gold coin,
While iguanas wear their shades,
In flip-flops they strut with flair,
Creating quite the tropical parades.

The parrot squawks a silly tune,
As tourists sip their fruity drinks,
They mimic every joke it tells,
The laughter flows like pastel inks.

Amidst the palms, a monkey swings,
With bananas tied like bows,
It juggles fruits and cracks some jokes,
Oh, the comedy that grows!

Rhythms of the Sun-Kissed Shore

Sandy toes and sunburned nose,
Laughter echoes where the tide flows.
Seagulls squawk, like they own the place,
Trying to steal my ice cream space.

Shells in pockets, hats askew,
Dancing dolphins, what a view!
Coconuts rolling, quite the show,
As I trip over, just for show!

Harmony Beneath the Stars

Under the moon, the crabs prance,
While the tourists try their dance.
Mango salsa in my hand,
A sticky mess, oh isn't it grand?

Stars above in perfect twirl,
I trip and stumble, give a whirl.
Hermit crabs join in the fun,
Who knew beach nights could weigh a ton?

The Dance of Colorful Wings

Butterflies flitter, in chaos and cheer,
Chasing the nectar, never too near.
I wave my arms, try to blend,
But they just laugh, not a friend!

Parrots gossip, squawk with flair,
As I fumble with my beach chair.
Sunburned backs, laughter on replay,
In the tropical fun, we drift away.

Echoes of a Coastal Dream

Waves crash in rhythmic delight,
Surfers tumble, oh what a sight!
My beach ball flies, has its own plan,
Bouncing off the hapless man.

Starfish sunbathe, don't seem to care,
While I juggle snacks, a messy affair.
As evening falls, we sing a tune,
To the beat of the waves and a laughing moon.

Echoing Through the Emerald Expanse

In the jungle, I lose my shoes,
Monkeys laugh, they sing the blues.
Parrots squawk in vibrant hues,
Who knew nature had such views?

With coconuts, I try to dance,
But trip and fall—oh, what a chance!
A lizard winks, gives me a glance,
Nature's got some awkward trance.

Serenade to the Sun-Kissed Shores

On sandy shores, my toes wiggle,
Crabs dance 'round, they really giggle.
A beach ball bounces, then it'll jiggle,
Watch out, my sunburn's starting to giggle!

Sunsets blaze, like paint on walls,
Lost my shoes—oh dear, where are they, y'all?
The tide rolls in, like nature's calls,
But seagulls swoop and steal my snacks, the brawls!

The Pulse of Palm-Studded Paradise

Under palms, the breeze is sweet,
Dancing lizards find their beat.
Sunburned noses, laughter neat,
Who knew the beach had such a feat?

Surfers wipe out, fall with a splash,
The ocean laughs, a comical crash.
But with each wave, they take a bash,
And friends cheer loud, it's quite the clash.

Delight in the Dappled Sunlight

In the shade, I sip my drink,
A squirrel steals my sandwich—what a link!
The sunbeams tickle, making me blink,
As laughter rolls, I start to think.

Butterflies flutter, all in line,
They gossip loud, call me divine.
Watch me trip over roots that entwine,
Yet here in joy, all hearts align.

Harmony Between the Stars and the Sea

The stars laugh above as waves twinkle bright,
A crab dances slow, what a curious sight.
Pelicans swoop down for a fishy delight,
While dolphins gossip, what a joyous night.

The moon wears a hat made of shimmering light,
Seagulls play poker and it's quite a fight.
The beach ball rolls away, what a silly flight,
While I am left wondering, where's my kite?

Anthem of the Exotic

A parrot in a hat sings tunes with flair,
While monkeys do yoga, without a care.
Coconut drinks served with umbrellas rare,
The sun plays peek-a-boo with perfect glare.

Hula skirts waving, oh what a show!
Sandcastles iffy, like a wobbly row.
Palm trees gossip in a breezy flow,
The lizards jump in, "Hey, let's go slow!"

Vision of the Verdant Isles

A turtle in shades suns under the rays,
While flamingos gossip in their own ways.
Banana peels slip, oh what a phase,
As the islanders dance through sun-soaked haze.

Mangoes are flying, oh what a scene!
Tropical breezes are breezy, you mean?
As giggling fruits roll on the green screen,
With laughter and fun, they make a great team!

Caress of the Coastal Breezes

The wind tells secrets to the sandy shore,
Where a crab struts around, wanting to explore.
Tide pool shenanigans, all wanting more,
Seashells giggle, "Let's have a score!"

Wave after wave, like laughter it flows,
With seaweed dancing in hilarious shows.
A beach ball escapes, oh where it goes,
Now the gulls are laughing, as everyone knows!

Poem of the Pebbled Shores

On pebbled shores, I stub my toe,
The waves return, with laughs in tow.
The crabs parade, a wobbly show,
While seagulls steal my chips, oh no!

Beneath the sun, my hat takes flight,
It flutters off, a silly sight.
The sunscreen's smeared, not quite right,
My nose is red, like a beacon's light.

Notes from the Nectar of Nature

The flowers giggle, bright and bold,
They tickle bees, a buzz so old.
The fruit bowl dances, green and gold,
And mango juice is pure liquid gold.

The monkeys swing, their jokes are cheesy,
They toss coconuts, they're feeling freezy.
A parrot squawks, but it's not easy,
To figure out if he's just being breezy.

Reverberations of the Rain

Raindrops tap like a drummer's beat,
I splash in puddles, oh what a treat!
The frogs leap high, they can't be beat,
While ducks waddle by, with flippers neat.

Umbrellas spin like tops in play,
As thunder grumbles, "Who wants to stay?"
Gods of mischief join the fray,
While puddles form a muddy ballet.

Ballad of the Beaches at Dusk

As twilight paints the sky in hues,
My beach chair calls, I can't refuse.
A seagull lands, and steals my views,
Then dives for fries, with its funny snooze.

The bonfire crackles, sparks do fly,
While awkward dancers give it a try.
Tomorrow's sun shines bright and spry,
But right now, laughter fills the sky.

Tropical Whispers in the Breeze

In the sun, the roosters crow,
Coconuts roll to and fro,
Lizards dance with a happy jig,
While the tourists take a swig.

Frisbees fly with all their might,
Even the iguanas take flight,
Umbrellas tip and drinks go wide,
As beach balls bounce like a wild ride.

Pineapples wear sunglasses neat,
With every wave, they can't be beat,
As the sandcastles start to sway,
Kids cry out, "Let's play all day!"

Sipping drinks with little umbrellas,
Mood's so light, we're all great fellas,
Laughter echoes through the trees,
In this paradise, we're all at ease.

Lush Melodies of Paradise

Bongo drums keep a steady beat,
While monkeys swing and dance on feet,
Parrots squawk with joy and flair,
As they steal our snacks, beware!

Watermelons roll down the hill,
Chasing friends who can't keep still,
Tropical fruits in a funny race,
Sticky hands and merry face.

It's a feast of colors so bright,
Tasting cake at the full moonlight,
Alligators grin from afar,
Snapping selfies—oh, what a star!

Chasing crabs with wiggly style,
We trip and laugh, it's worth the while,
In this land of laughter and light,
Every moment feels just right.

Ocean's Lullaby at Dawn

The sun peeks over ocean blue,
A sleeping dolphin yawns too,
Seagulls gossip, oh what fun,
As they chase the rolling sun.

Sandcastles brave the morning waves,
While crabby friends just misbehave,
Tides wash in with funny tunes,
And starfish dance beneath the moons.

Shells gather secrets from the sea,
Whispering tales to you and me,
A clam tries hard to sing along,
But it holes up—it can't be strong.

With laughter ringing through the sands,
We build high towers with our hands,
And as the day starts to unfold,
Ocean stories will be retold.

Serenade of the Palm Trees

Palm trees sway, they sing and sway,
Tickled by wind in a playful play,
Coconuts drop, a thud on the ground,
While cheeky squirrels race around.

Bamboo shoots shoot up with pride,
As playful shadows seek to hide,
Hammocks swing with a jiggle and bounce,
While we sip drinks with a happy founce.

Laughter bubbles like a bright brook,
As colorful fish put on a hook,
A crab steals lunch on a daring spree,
Yelling 'Hey, come catch me if you please!'

The sun dips low with a cheeky grin,
As we gather for laughter and din,
In this place where every breeze hums,
Funny tales of the tropics come.

Lullabies of the Lush Canopy

In the trees where monkeys swing,
They dance and laugh, oh what a fling.
A parrot squawks a silly rhyme,
While iguanas chill, having a good time.

Beneath the leaves, a sloth does yawn,
Dreaming of snacks and the break of dawn.
A chipmunk perched with acorn stash,
Says, 'I'm quite ready for my next big splash!'

The breeze carries laughter on its way,
As the bright sun shimmies in the day.
All creatures join this merry beat,
In a canopy where fun and giggles meet.

So let's sway to the jungle's tune,
Under the watch of a lazy moon.
With every nook and every twist,
Join the choir of fun, you can't resist!

Serenade in Sunset Hues

As the sun dips low and paints the sky,
A toucan jokes, 'Do you even fly?'
Palm trees sway, they join the jest,
Their shadows dancing, it's just the best.

With coconuts dropping, what a thrill,
Each one hits the ground with a silly spill.
Laughter echoes as gulls take flight,
In this twilight scene, everything feels right.

A sea breeze whispers jokes from afar,
Conch shells join in, a musical star.
Under skies of orange and pink,
Nature's comedy makes us think!

So grab a friend and give a cheer,
In hues of sunset, we shed a tear.
For life's a joke, but oh so sweet,
With echoes of laughter, we dance on our feet!

Melodies of the Ocean Breeze

Waves ripple with a playful cheer,
Where dolphins flip and dolphins leer.
The seagulls squawk their cheeky tales,
As fish jump high, wearing shiny scales.

A crab does the cha-cha, quite a sight,
While starfish giggle in their own light.
The sun dips low, reflecting each grin,
In this ocean's party, let the fun begin!

Shells play tambourines along the shore,
While sea turtles tap—it's a dance encore.
With artists of sandcraft in their zone,
Each grain of sand writes jokes of their own.

So raise your voice and sing quite loud,
For the ocean's fun makes us all proud.
In breezy moments, laughter flows,
Embrace the whimsy, let joy impose!

Rhythm of the Rainforest

In a rainforest where the frogs all croak,
They laugh at the mist, 'Ahh, what a joke!'
Slipping on leaves, a sloth takes a spill,
While toucans chuckle, giving a thrill.

The vines swing low with a playful grin,
A monkey swings high—let the fun begin!
Drip-drop raindrops turn into a beat,
As the forest dances on muddy street.

A beat provided by the crickets' hum,
And a tap dancer ant gets everyone numb.
With each leafy note, we sway with cheer,
In this vibrant tune, it's perfectly clear.

So revel in laughter, let worries fade,
In the rhythm of life, a grand parade.
For laughter echoes in every tone,
In the rainforest, we celebrate the unknown!

Harmony of Heavens and Horizons

In a hammock swinging wide,
Two monkeys throw a slide.
Bananas fall like rain,
Adding to their silly gain.

The sun wears shades of gold,
While stories, loud and bold.
Palm trees sway in the breeze,
Laughing 'til they bend their knees.

A toucan sings a silly tune,
Dance partners with the moon.
Bellyflops in the sea,
Splash echoes with glee.

A crab wears a tiny hat,
Dancing with a sleeping cat.
In this tropical delight,
Every laugh takes flight.

Rhapsody of Raindrops

Raindrops tap on leaves with glee,
Dancing frogs, one, two, three!
Underneath their leafy roof,
Wiggly worms join in the goof.

A parrot squawks a soggy jest,
While puddles host a jolly fest.
Rubber ducks float near the shore,
Singing songs of rain galore.

The sky gives a cheeky grin,
As lightning starts to spin.
Clouds throw a drizzly cheer,
While kids jump in, oh dear!

Belly flops in muddy pools,
Splashing while the rain just drools.
With each drop a giggle swells,
Nature's voice, a song that tells.

The Dance of the Fireflies

Fireflies twinkle, quite the show,
As nighttime steals the glow.
They form a jolly conga line,
Zigzagging in a sweet design.

A frog joins in the merry dance,
Thinking this is his big chance.
He trips over a leafy sprout,
And all the lights begin to shout!

Crickets play on tiny strings,
While mischief in the twilight clings.
With winks and pips, they weave around,
Creating laughs without a sound.

As the moon laughs big and bright,
The fireflies twirl, what a sight!
A blend of giggles, light, and fun,
In the dance, they've just begun.

Chords of the Coastal Night

The waves hum a silly tune,
Beneath the stars and cheeky moon.
Seashells giggle on the shore,
As crabs dance, wanting more.

A seaspray sprays a fishy kiss,
While dolphins playfully twist.
They leap up high, such joyful sights,
Turning tides with merry flights.

Coconuts roll, having their say,
In this coastal cabaret.
With sandy toes and salty hair,
Everyone joins without a care.

As night winds play their mellow chords,
Laughter spills like sunny hoards.
Together, they serenade the night,
In this coastal scene of delight.

Ode to the Solstice Sun

Oh, blazing ball of golden cheer,
You roast my skin, yet bring me beer.
Your rays are great for grillin' franks,
But oh, how I forget my thanks.

You roast the ants upon the sand,
And turn my toes to crisp demand.
The seagulls laugh, they steal my fries,
While I just sunbathe and disguise.

With each sweet drink, I lose my thoughts,
My brain's on vacation, tied in knots.
I dance with joy, I trip on shells,
Thus, in this heat, hilarity dwells.

So here's to you, dear scorching ball,
For laughs, for fun, you bring us all.
Through sweat and smiles, we'll sing your song,
A jest in sun, all day long.

Constellations Over Tropical Waters

When evening falls, the stars appear,
A sparkling dance, a cosmic leer.
I lie on my float, a buoyed mess,
And ponder things that I confess.

Is that a fish or a star I see?
Or simply the glow of my last piña colada spree?
Venus winks, as if to tease,
While I splash about, just aim to please.

The moon beams down with silvery glow,
I chase my dreams, maybe catch a toe.
With every swell, a giggle escapes,
As jellyfish morph into grape-shaped shapes.

In this warm night, I must insist,
Every splash is a wave of bliss.
So raise a toast to the twinkling fun,
Under the laughing light of the moonlit run.

Portrait of the Pristine Beach

On the canvas of sand, my footprints play,
Each step a dance in the ocean's ballet.
I build a castle, it leans and falls,
While seagulls plot my snack-time brawls.

The waves retreat, then pull me in,
Salty kisses turn to sun-kissed skin.
Each grain of sand, a secret spy,
That tickles my toes as time flutters by.

I sip a drink from a coconut cup,
While tiny crabs dance, never give up.
The sun's a painter, with strokes so bright,
Leaving my hat to fly like a kite.

So here's to fun on this sunny shore,
Where laughter bubbles, and spirits soar.
In nature's gallery, let funny prevail,
On this beach where all troubles sail.

Verses of the Vibrating Vines

Twisted green with laughter loud,
The vines dance wildly, a toucan crowd.
They sway and wiggle, they move with glee,
They challenge the waves to join their spree.

I swing from fronds, like Tarzan does,
But end up tangled, without a buzz.
With each bold leap, I touch the sky,
And land in mud, oh me, oh my!

The monkeys cheer, with playful grins,
As I wear leaves like hats for wins.
The jungle hums a funny tune,
Encouraging me to bounce like a balloon.

So let's embrace the vines today,
And laugh out loud in our own way.
For in this jungle, IDeclare it fine,
You'll find your joy in every vine!

Synthesis of Sun and Sea

The sun puts on a golden hat,
While crabs dance like they're in a spat.
Fish sing songs in giddy delight,
As dolphins plan their next big flight.

Coconuts bounce in rhythmic beats,
Tickling toes of tourists on heats.
Laughter spills like lemonade bright,
While seagulls steal fries, what a sight!

The Tides' Tender Caress

Waves sneak up like they're playing tag,
Splashing smiles, oh what a brag!
Shells gather giggles from the shore,
As seaweed here does a funky chore.

Crab races held at the edge so bold,
With spectators that won't fold.
The tide winks, splashing without fuss,
While sandcastle kings argue, 'What's a plus?'

Stanzas of Sacred Rain

Raindrops tap dance on palm leaves green,
A slippery stage, a tropical scene.
Umbrellas flip like they're a shoe,
While puddles become ponds just for two.

Frogs croak choruses in a grand show,
The sky grumbles jokes we can't outgrow.
With every drop, a giggle, a grin,
As the sunshine waits for its turn to win.

Whimsical Waves and Whispering Winds

Whispers float in the salty air,
As kites dance without a care.
The wind tells tales of silly days,
While surfers carve their watery maze.

Turtles race on a curious quest,
To find the best sunbathing nest.
With each breeze, joy takes a spin,
Tropical laughter sails on a whim.

Echoes of Island Dreams

In the market, a parrot steals,
Fruit from stalls, oh what a deal!
Dancing crabs steal the show,
Wiggly tails, putting on a glow.

Lazy sun, but the roosters crow,
Chasing shadows, they scatter and go.
Tropical breezes tickle your face,
While you run in a flip-flop race.

Coconuts fall like heavy bombs,
Splitting smiles, causing giddy qualms.
Kids in the wave, catching a ride,
Splashing about with nothing to hide.

Under palm trees with swings so grand,
Lizards plotting their mischievous plan.
A hammock swings low, holding tight,
Dreaming of belly laughs through the night.

Harmonics of Hibiscus Blooms

Bumblebees in a flower fight,
Chasing around till the fall of night.
Hibiscus laughs, sways in the breeze,
Dropping petals like tiny cheesy keys.

Swaying palms play a funny tune,
Boys trying to surf on a silver moon.
Floaties pop with a giggle and glee,
Splashing in puddles, as wild as can be.

The sun wears shades, looks oh so cool,
While kids compete for the silliest pool.
Mermaids gossip, their tails a blur,
Chasing fish that pretend they stir.

Kites made of dreams, colors so bright,
Lifted by wind in the tropical light.
Our laughter echoes beneath the skies,
With each silly glance, mischief lies.

Chants Under the Mango Tree

Under the mango, gossip flows,
Squirrels wear hats, striking silly poses.
An old tortoise sings with glee,
Attracting crabs, a wild jubilee.

The coconuts laugh with a mighty thud,
Rolling down hills like a playful bud.
Banana peels fly through the air,
Witty tricks that bring on the flair.

Giggling children chase after dreams,
Painting the sky with fantastical schemes.
A frog conducts from a lily pad,
Creating symphonies that make us glad.

Caught by the wind, a kite takes flight,
Twisting and turning in sheer delight.
While shadows dance to the mango's beat,
Every laugh is a tropical treat.

Dances with the Dusk Air

As the sun dips in a fiery swirl,
Seashells giggle, and oceans twirl.
Teenage dolphins put on a show,
Surfing the waves with a splash and a throw.

There's a dance organized by the breeze,
Where flip-flops tango, making us tease.
Gusts of wind hold back our hair,
While seagulls squawk at our funny flair.

Lanterns light up the night sky,
While mosquitoes buzz and hover by.
A firefly leads with a flickering guide,
In the rhythm of laughter, we all slide.

Palm trees sway, joining the cheer,
Offering coconuts, festive and near.
Under the stars, we groove and prance,
In tropical nights, we all take a chance.

Tones of the Timeless Tropics

In a hammock, I do sway,
My worries drift away,
Sipping coconut delight,
While mosquitoes dance in flight.

Lizards chase the falling sun,
A lizard and I, we have fun,
He struts with a funky flair,
I can't help but stop and stare.

The parrot squawks, 'No more cake!',
I told him, 'Buddy, make no mistake!'
He laughs too loud, I must confess,
Together, we wear quite the mess.

On the beach, I trip and fall,
Crabs all laugh, it's quite the brawl,
But in this sunny, silly scene,
I find joy, forever keen.

Mystical Chants of the South Seas

The waves sing songs, oh so bright,
A fishy choir, what a sight!
Gulls join the tune, loud and proud,
While walruses dance, oh so loud.

With a coconut hat, I parade,
The island's stage, I'm not afraid,
The pineapple's winking at me,
As I salsa with a palm tree.

Down by the shores, a crab takes flight,
He tumbles and rolls, quite the sight!
The seaweed giggles along the shore,
Oh, the ocean's funny encore!

When the sun dips, we wild locals jest,
Telling tales of the fish's quest,
With laughter echoing through the night,
The South Seas sing, what pure delight!

Cascading Sounds of the Cascades

Echoes bounce through the thick green,
As monkeys swing, they're quite the scene,
Splashing in puddles, they skit and play,
Nature's circus, hip-hip-hooray!

The waterfall roars, a giddy shout,
A frog jumps high, flinging about,
I slip on moss, fall with grace,
Now I'm part of this wild race!

The bamboo laughs in the gentle breeze,
As I dance by the honeybees,
All together in this joyful jest,
The woodland chuckles, it's the best!

Underneath the palms, I make a stand,
Trying to juggle with shell in hand,
The forest chortles, what a sight,
With soundscapes that spark pure delight!

The Omnipresent Ocean's Whisper

The ocean winks with a playful wave,
Tickling toes, oh, how they misbehave!
Seashells giggle, a hidden laugh,
Under waves that dance and quaff.

Dolphins' chatter fills the blue,
Singing songs to me and you,
They leap like dancers in the sun,
Making mischief, oh what fun!

Starfish gossip on warm sandy beds,
While crabs wear crowns, and greet their dreads,
I try to join their royal parade,
But fall right in, oh, what charade!

As night blankets the shimmering sea,
The ocean whispers, 'Come and see!'
With a flick of light, the laughter rings,
In this world of joy, where fun never swings.

Tranquil Tides and Shimmering Sights

Palm trees sway, they dance so sleek,
A crab in shorts, I hear it speak.
Waves tickle toes, the sun's a tease,
Seagulls mock, yet bring us ease.

Dolphins prank with flips so bright,
They salute the sun, what a sight!
Shells that giggle on the sand,
Who knew nature had a band?

Sunburned noses look so proud,
Sunhats fly in winds, quite loud.
Beach balls bounce, a playing fight,
Laughter echoes 'til the night.

Flip-flops flung, a mischief spree,
Tropical joys, come play with me!
A juicy mango, what a dream,
Life's a wild, fruity theme!

The Colorful Serenade of Nature

Parrots sing in hues so bright,
Each color pops, a pure delight.
Lizards lounge, so cool and sly,
A butterfly flirts, oh my, oh my!

Coconuts drop with hefty thuds,
While ants march in tiny floods.
Mango trees don their best strut,
As chipmunks munch, they take a cut.

Giggles echo from leaves above,
Nature's joy, the wildest love.
Sunshine winks, a playful jest,
In this canvas, we feel blessed.

Hammocks swing, the laughter flies,
With quirky clouds in painted skies.
Nature's serenade, so absurd,
A symphony without a word!

Twilight Over Golden Sands

As the sun dips, it waves goodbye,
Sandcastles sigh with a sleepy eye.
Shadows stretch, the crabs come out,
Under the stars, it's time to shout!

A beach ball rolls, a ghostly race,
Tidal whispers, a soft embrace.
Fireflies blink in a winking spree,
While beachgoers dance with glee.

Chill vibes flow like ocean's breeze,
Funny tales bring us to our knees.
Seashells chatter, what a show,
In tonight's glow, we let it flow!

Twilight dances with a gentle tease,
Each moment savored, life's sweet breeze.
Laughter lingers like a feather,
Paradise found, now and forever!

Whispers of the Forgotten Cove

In the cove where treasures hide,
Old pirates chuckle, filled with pride.
Seashells gossip, sharing news,
While treasure maps play coy and snooze.

Beneath the waves, a turtle rolls,
Giggles bubble from tidal shoals.
Algae wiggles, a dance of fun,
While octopuses give a pun!

Forgotten tales beneath the tide,
Mermaids join, they laugh and glide.
Fish in bow ties swim with grace,
Making time in this secret place.

Cove's secrets wrapped in salty mist,
Every wave a playful twist.
With minor mischief, all will coo,
In this haven, we'll start anew!

Verses of the Vibrant Lagoon

In the lagoon, the fish do dance,
Wearing tiny hats, they prance.
A crab sings loud, a tuneful jest,
With his claws, he plays the best.

The frogs wear shades, they croak with flair,
Riding lily pads without a care.
The water's bright, a swirling green,
Who knew a pond could be so keen?

A turtle spins in joyful glee,
Sipping cocktails made from sea.
A parrot shares the gossip now,
While sea cucumbers take a bow.

With laughter echoing all around,
The vibrant life in waves is found.
In this lagoon, the fun's not shy,
Just ask the fish who wear ties high!

Mood of the Moonlit Beach

On moonlit sands, the crabs parade,
In flip-flops worn, their plans are laid.
They wiggle, dance, and laugh with cheer,
Attempting moonwalks, quite sincere.

A starfish joins, a suave old chap,
With shades at night, he takes a nap.
Shells sing out, a gentle tune,
While jellyfish float under the moon.

Sandcastles grow, designed with heart,
A moat of sea, a work of art.
A clam declares its royal claim,
While seagulls join, they're in the game!

The waves high-five the shore so grand,
As laughter spills across the sand.
In this bright night where dreams can breach,
Silly funny whispers on the beach.

Sonnet for Statuesque Sand Dunes

The dunes stand tall, like giants bold,
Whispering secrets of time untold.
With grains that shift, they dance and sway,
In breezy gusts, they laugh and play.

A lizard struts, a tiny king,
In a crown of twigs, he feels the zing.
While tumbleweeds roll with glee,
Declaring dance-offs; come witness me!

Seagulls circle, cawing just right,
Challenging clouds to a silly flight.
And cacti sway, they take a bow,
Announcing the sunset's vibrant wow!

The sands chuckle, they shift and tease,
A playful muse that aims to please.
Together we share, beneath the moons,
With whispers of joy, in sandy tunes.

Cadence of the Coral Gardens

In coral gardens, colors flash bright,
Like a painter's palette in pure delight.
Fish twirl about in a funky show,
While anemones wave with a friendly glow.

A clownfish jester, with antics galore,
Tells seaweed tales that make us roar.
Seahorses sway in a dreamy trance,
While star corals host an underwater dance.

The sea turtle tells the silliest rhyme,
About swimming fast—at a snail's time.
Octopuses play with eightfold grace,
As bubbles rise in a playful chase.

From vibrant depths to shoreline's hum,
The coral calls, here comes the fun!
Together we laugh, forever we'll play,
In this magic realm, come join the sway!

Vibrations of a Tropical Storm

The clouds danced like they're at a ball,
Raindrops tap-danced down the hall,
A parrot squawks with flair and zest,
While the palm trees sway, they do their best.

The winds shout jokes, both wild and loud,
As coconut drinks spill on the crowd,
Flip-flops flying, a grand parade,
In this stormy spree, sunshine's delayed.

Lightning giggles, thunder snickers,
Nature's own comedian, pulling the flickers,
In puddles, the kids make boats of leaves,
While the storm's energy perfectly weaves.

Just when the downpour seems to decline,
Rainbows pop up, oh so divine,
A tropical storm? Such a wild jest,
Who knew nature could party like the best?

Spheres of Serenity and Surfer's Surges

Waves crash forth like they're on a spree,
Surfers giggle, "Look, that's me!"
With boards like rockets, they glide and flip,
While fish below do a synchronized trip.

Sand castles rise like towers so proud,
Until a rogue wave brings a crowd,
"Oops," they say, as the towers fall,
Beachside laughter echoes, a carnival call.

The sun grins wide, baking us toast,
As seagulls swoop in, who needs a host?
"Free snacks!" they squawk, in swooping delight,
While beachballs soar way into the night.

Ocean whispers secrets to the tide,
As evening settles, we swim and slide,
With stars overhead, and laughter in air,
This tropical ballet, beyond compare.

Interlude of the Island's Heartbeat

The island pulses with a bouncy beat,
Palm trees groove, shuffling their feet,
Coconuts grin, they roll around,
While hula dancers spin on the ground.

In the distance, a ukulele sings,
As crabs do the cha-cha, with tiny things,
Flip-flops clapping, a rhythm divine,
As laughter erupts, in a sunny line.

Glimmers of sunlight play hide and seek,
A pineapple stands, looking quite chic,
With smiles so broad, the fun never stops,
While sea turtles dance with joyful hops.

When the sun dips low, a party ignites,
With firefly twinkles and sparkling lights,
The island's heartbeat, playful and bright,
Keeps rolling on through this magical night.

The Language of Frangipani Nights

Frangipani blooms with scents so sweet,
Under the moon, the night feels complete,
Laughter drifts on the warm, gentle breeze,
As friends share tales, with such perfect ease.

In the shadows, the crickets compose,
With every chirp, a symphony grows,
Coconut cups filled with cheer and glee,
While the stars wink, like they're in on the key.

Dancing shadows beneath the sway,
Where every giggle and jest holds sway,
In this land where the rules are few,
Frangipani nights, we embrace the new.

With dreams taking flight on the wings of the air,
Each moment a treasure, precious and rare,
When the world is a stage, laughter's the gist,
In this amusing paradise, how could we resist?

The Gentle Wave's Tune

The waves come in with a wobbly dance,
Doing the cha-cha, as if in a trance.
They tickle our toes as they crash and sway,
Oh, what a silly, splashy ballet!

A dolphin pops up, grinning with glee,
He joins in the fun, he's got quite the spree.
With flips and splashes, he steals the show,
Making us laugh till our sides overflow!

Palm trees sway gently, they join the tune,
With rustling leaves like a jazzy cartoon.
They wiggle and jiggle under the sun,
These goofy old palms know how to have fun!

So let's raise a toast to these waves that play,
And dance 'til the sunset takes us away.
In this tropical realm, where the laughter swells,
We'll snorkel the sea and ring those bells!

Echoing Laughter in Tropical Air.

In the bright sun, we are all silly fools,
Chasing crabs that think they're swimming schools.
With laughter echoing, we frolic about,
Who knew beach days could bring such a shout!

A parrot squawks jokes with a cheeky flair,
As we sip on drinks with a colorful stare.
"Polly wants laughter!" he cackles with pride,
We can't stop giggling, we're beaming wide!

The sandcastles lean with a whimsical bend,
As our buckets and pails collide and blend.
"Moat? Who needs that?" A wave sweeps them back,
The tide plays tricks, our plans go off track!

But even the sun seems to chuckle and glow,
Winking at us with a warm, teasing throw.
As the stars join the fun, lighting up the night,
We dance through the shadows, oh what a sight!

Tropical Symphony

The sun plays a tune on the ocean's bright skin,
While surfboards and giggles mix with a grin.
Turtles in tuxedos glide by with flair,
Conducting the waves, they make quite a pair!

The ukulele strums as the lizards dance round,
And flip-flops are drumming on sandy ground.
With each funny step, the coconuts chuckle,
As the sun sets slowly, it's pure tropical huddle!

A crab plays the maracas, all clack and no cue,
While fish blow bubbles and join in the hue.
Even the clouds join this wacky parade,
Raining laughter instead of a cascade!

As the day slips away, a new song will rise,
With subtle giggles and glorious sighs.
In this merry paradise, under stars that twine,
We find joy in chaos, yeah, that suits us just fine!

Whispers of the Coconut Palm

Coconuts chime in, with a gentle sway,
"I've got a joke, care to join in the play?"
As they tumble down from their lofty throne,
We laugh so hard, we forget the unknown!

The breezy winds carry our chuckles away,
Tickling the sea and the vibrant bay.
Each wave whispers secrets, all bubbly and bright,
While we chase the sunsets, in pure delight.

The flip-flops are dancing, doing a jig,
As we spin and twirl, just feeling so big!
The fireflies join with their sparkly cheer,
Together we pretend that there's nothing to fear!

Let's toast to the laughter, under stars that gleam,
In this wild land of whispers, we dance in a dream.
With each silly moment and giggle we share,
We know in this paradise, life's free as the air!

Sweet Lament of the Mango Tree

Oh, juicy mango, wearing green attire,
You dangle from branches, a sweet desire.
But down below, a goat wanders near,
He snickers and munches, oh what a fear!

When summer arrives, you drop with a thud,
The kids cheer aloud, 'Look, fruit in the mud!'
Yet, mangos they squish, with giggles and glee,
While I stand there grumbling, 'Who's laughing at me?'

Your nectar so rich, my heart skips a beat,
Yet their messy fingertips, oh such a defeat!
They leave me in ruins, my skin all a mess,
But I still bear witness, their sticky success.

With each sunny day, I sway in the breeze,
As laughter erupts, it's the wildest of fees.
Though my branches may ache, and my bark may feel sore,
I chuckle and sigh, for I'm loved evermore.

Crescendo of the Tropical Storm

Here comes the storm, with a thunderous roar,
The palm trees all dance, while the pitter-pats pour.
A parrot squawks loudly, 'Hold on to your hat!'
While the dog on the porch just splashes and chats.

Raindrops like marbles, they roll down the lane,
Slipping and sliding, they just can't contain.
The kids pull boats made from leaves and some string,
Pretending they're captains, oh the joy that they bring!

Oh, but there's chaos, the chickens all flee,
Chasing their shadows, as wet as can be.
The winds whirl and twirl, like a wild carnival,
While I grin in my roots, oh, the weirdness of all!

Once the water recedes, we breathe out a sigh,
Sunshine breaks through, painting rainbows on high.
Drenched but quite happy, we clean up the streets,
And toast to the storm with our wiggly feet.

Nectar of the Sunlit Splendor

Oh nectar so bright in the lemony light,
It sparkles and winks, what a stunning sight!
But those buzzing bees think I'm some sort of snack,
They buzz like they're royalty, ready to attack.

I stand here adorned, in blossoms so fine,
While ants climb my stalks, in search of a dine.
They march with a purpose, a delightful parade,
All while I giggle, their plans have been laid!

A tortoise ambles near, dreaming of feast,
He eyes my sweet fruits, oh what a beast!
But while he's so slow, and I'm swift on my feet,
I'll bounce to the zinnias, oh, life is a treat!

As night starts to fall, the fireflies bloom,
I dance in the twilight, in the softest of gloom.
Life here is charming, with nature's grand song,
In this sunlit splendor, all senses belong.

Paradise's Soliloquy

In the heart of the island, where coconuts sway,
I ponder the joy of each whimsical day.
A crab scuttles by with a curious glance,
While I hum to the rhythm of life's merry dance.

The sun teases gently, as shadows grow long,
Catching the breeze in a jovial song.
My friends, the lizards, they share their wise tale,
Of mischief and mayhem, as they wiggle and flail.

But oh let's not forget, the ants on parade,
Their diligent hustle, a spectacle made.
They march to their rhythm, a tiny brigade,
While I watch and chuckle, at their grand charade.

A toucan calls out, 'Achtung, beware!'
As I spill my drink and join in the affair.
In this paradise glow, we share every laugh,
In nature's grand scheme, we write our own path.

Journey Through the Jungle Canopy

Swinging high with monkeys bold,
They steal the fruit, or so I'm told.
Parrots squawk a playful tune,
While snakes dance 'neath a glowing moon.

Frogs croak jokes that make you grin,
As if they're trying to win a spin.
Lemurs leap like bouncy springs,
In this place, oh, joy it brings!

Vines entwine like friends at play,
A lizard gives a wild display.
Giggling bugs dance in the air,
A comedy show without a care.

Treetops sway with laughter bright,
In this canopy, pure delight.
So come along, don't be shy,
Let's swing and laugh until we fly!

Lull of the Land and Sea

Waves crash softly on the shore,
Seagulls squawk; they crave for more.
Crabs do jiggy little shuffles,
While jellyfish float and do their hustles.

Sunsets paint a golden scene,
While dolphins tease, it's quite serene.
A turtle with a sunburned shell,
Says, 'I've got a funny tale to tell!'

The breeze whispers sweet silly rhymes,
As fish perform their underwater crimes.
Scuba divers laugh like crazy,
In fishy fashions, feeling hazy.

With a coconut drink held high,
We toast to laughs 'neath the open sky.
For land and sea create this blend,
A lull of joy that knows no end!

A Canvas of Colors and Calls

Brushes dipped in ocean hues,
Nature's palette gives us cues.
Flamingos prance in pastel works,
While toucans chuckle with goofy quirks.

Green is bold in every leaf,
As sloths move slow, beyond belief.
A painted frog with polka dots,
Sings off-key in silly spots.

Nightfall brings a disco glow,
With fireflies putting on a show.
Creatures wear their night attire,
A canvas bright, never to tire.

Laughter echoes through the trees,
While night birds join in harmonies.
In this vibrant, joyful thrall,
How can we not love it all?

The Rhythms of Rainforest Souls

Drum beats echo, woodpeckers chime,
Makeshift bands in leafy clime.
Beetles tap in rhythm true,
While frogs keep time, as good friends do.

In this beat, a parrot croons,
As monkeys sway to merry tunes.
Each creature joins the joyful beat,
With sounds that dance beneath our feet.

The humidity hums a bass,
While lizards dash with speedy grace.
A snake slides by, with a wink and a nod,
Saying, 'Don't tread on this little odd!'

Moods swing like branches in the breeze,
As laughter flows with perfect ease.
Oh, these rhythms, naughty delight,
Make our jungle nights feel just right!

Breath of the Bountiful Tropics

The coconuts fell with a thud,
My hat flew off, oh what a dud!
The parrot squawked, a silly prank,
As I dodged jungle juice from the tank.

Lizards danced on my sunburned toes,
While monkeys played peekaboo through the throes.
I slipped on a mango, went head over heels,
And landed right in the turf that's for meals.

The waves laughed hard as they rolled on the shore,
A crab tiptoed by and then asked for more.
With a wink and a grin on its armored face,
It challenged me to a crustacean race!

The breeze brought scents, oh so exotic,
I sneezed, and my friends found it chaotic.
They laughed as I flailed with pollen-filled glee,
Who knew such mischief could come from a tree?

Tapestry of Tropical Twilight

The sun dips low, painting skies like dreams,
In my hammock I swing, or so it seems.
But a mosquito buzzes, the prankster flies,
Dancing 'round my ear—oh, how time flies!

A pineapple piña brings a bubbly cheer,
But spills on my shirt; my friends are near.
They snicker and chortle, it's quite a sight,
I'm sticky and sweet, oh what a delight!

The stars come out, twinkling like mad,
And I trip on a root, how utterly bad!
A firefly giggles, lighting my path,
As I dance with the dusk, just let out a laugh.

In this grand stage where the night calls out,
Tropics of joy are what it's about.
With coconuts laughing and palm trees swaying,
Who knew that mischief was so much playing?

Poetic Pulse of the Paradise Inhabitants

The toucan honked with a hilarious flair,
As I tried to walk in my flip-flops bare.
A crab on my left, a lizard on right,
Both critters were ready for a comical fight.

I joined in their tussle, what a silly spree,
My laughter echoed through the palm-lit spree.
Then a turtle ambled, quite slow and sly,
Giving a smirk as I zoomed on by.

Frogs croaked a rhythm, a funny little song,
While I hopped along, it felt all wrong!
My legs went astray, like a wobbly toy,
I crashed in the mud—oh joy, oh boy!

The night was alive with giggles and glee,
As the moon shone bright on this raucous spree.
The paradise folks joined in the fun,
In a dance of delight 'til the morning sun.

The Language of Lush Landscapes

In a garden where giggles bloom and play,
I met a chubby sloth who waved all day.
He said, "Don't hurry, take your time,"
As I tripped on my shoelaces, oh, what a crime!

The banana trees chuckled, their fruits held tight,
As I marched by boldly in pure delight.
But fell on my face with a slip and a slide,
The owls hooted loud, oh what a ride!

The flowers spun tales of humor and cheer,
While a bee whispered jokes, sweetened with beer.
We shared all our laughs 'neath the coconut shade,
A comedy show as the daylight did fade.

With laughter as music, the leaves joined the tune,
The jungle erupted with joy 'neath the moon.
Oh, in these green lands, where mischief unwinds,
The whispers of laughter are all that one finds.

Reverie Beneath the Palm Fronds

Under palm fronds, I lay and dream,
A coconut falls, what a silly theme!
Sunburnt toes, a mismatched tan,
Squawking parrots, the dance of a fan.

Sipping fruit punch, I spill on my shirt,
Laughter erupts like a playful alert.
The waves giggle as they roll to the shore,
While crabs play tag, oh what's in store!

A lizard struts by, a confident chap,
Winks at the sun, takes a little nap.
With a flip-flop fight against the breeze,
I join the ruckus, oh please, oh please!

Falling asleep with a grin on my face,
Dreaming of tacos in this sunny place.
The tropics tease with their sunlit glee,
Where every moment is a giggle spree.

Soliloquy of the Sapphire Seas

Waves in sunglasses, they splash and gleam,
Jellyfish pirouette, like fish in a dream.
Shells laugh, they tickle my curious toes,
While dolphins jest with their oceanic prose.

An octopus juggles a forgotten flip-flop,
And I can't decide if I want to stop.
Each wave whispers a salty delight,
As the sun has a chuckle, saying, 'What a sight!'

Seagulls debate if they should dive down,
To steal my snack; they're the kings of this town.
With chips in my hand, I defend my feast,
While crabs throw a party, they're wild, to say the least!

At sunset, the water winks at the skies,
And I snicker at fish in their hilarious ties.
The tropics are a stage for a slapstick act,
Where laughter and joy are perfectly packed.

Vibes of the Verdant Wilderness

In the jungle's embrace, vines take a swing,
Monkeys throw coconuts, oh what a fling!
Parrots discuss the latest gossip in trees,
While chameleons chuckle in hues with such ease.

A toucan struts, with a beak that's a blast,
Sipping on nectar, it's partying fast.
The sloths pass remarks about speed and grace,
While I'm stuck tripping on roots, what a race!

With frogs in tuxedos, they croak a fine tune,
Beware of the snake, who's planning a swoon.
The plants all dance to the breeze's soft song,
And I join in the fun; won't last long!

As twilight descends, the sounds become great,
The jungle's a band hosting its wild fate.
Each critter conspires, sets the stage for cheer,
In the vibrant wilderness, joy is so near.

Twilight Serenade by the Shore

Twilight approaches, a whimsical hue,
Crickets compose tunes, for me and for you.
Sandcastles sway, with a funny little bow,
While sea turtles emerge, oh this glorious show.

Seaweed dances, a long green dress,
As I trip in the sand, I must confess.
A starfish giggles, it's quite the sight,
"It's all in good fun!" it shouts with delight.

The moon starts to laugh, glowing bright and round,
Shells start to chirp, what strange little sounds!
The breeze carries whispers of stories untold,
As I'm swept away in this jesting gold.

With each wave that crashes, there's laughter anew,
In twilight's embrace, fun is the cue.
The shoreline is where all troubles may cease,
As joy spills over like the waves, piece by piece.

Silhouettes of Sundrenched Serenity

Sunshine creeps on golden feet,
Laughter dances, oh so sweet.
Coconuts fall, a thud and roll,
Watch your head or fear the toll!

Flip-flops flying, toes in sand,
Sunburnt noses, quite unplanned.
Tropic drinks in hands we sip,
Waves applaud our merry trip!

Hammocks sway with lazy grace,
Swaying to the sun's embrace.
Parrots chatter, they just can't stop,
"Where's the party? Right on top!"

When the day gives way to night,
Fireflies twinkle, what a sight!
We toast to mischief, wild and free,
In this paradise, come and see!

Canzone of the Coastal Flora

Flowers bloom with vivid flair,
Sun-baked petals without a care.
One wore sandals, oh what a sight,
Strutting proudly in morning light!

Sunflowers gossip, wild and loud,
Making jokes beneath the cloud.
"Why so bright?" they giggle near,
"Cuz we drink sunshine, hold your beer!"

Cacti frown, their spines on guard,
"Don't mess with us, it's quite hard!"
A daisy grinned, "I'm feeling bold!"
"Let's start a dance, let stories unfold!"

A rose chimed in, with petals twirled,
"Let's show this beach, a floral world!"
And in that moment, joy took flight,
In the warm glow of the twilight!

Ballad of the Bounty-Hunter Seas

Pirates laugh with treasure maps,
"Where's the gold?" they call with claps.
Sailing on a shrimp-boat dream,
Eating fish sticks, what a theme!

Seagulls squawk, a squabble loud,
"Yo-ho-ho, we're too proud!"
One lost a hat, a captain's fate,
Tossed to waves - let's celebrate!

Fish in shades of pink and green,
Dancing under waves unseen.
"Catch us if you dare, good luck!"
They flip and flop, a fishy pluck!

The sun sinks low, the crew's in cheer,
"Bring out the snacks and icy beer!"
With salty tales and guffaws wide,
In bounty seas, we'll laugh and glide!

Love Letters to the Lagoon

Whispers float on lagoon's breeze,
"Dear Lagoon, you've brought us ease."
Frogs croak songs of passionate flair,
Promising love, oh they declare!

Mossy rocks wearing their best,
Dance with waves, they never rest.
"Can you feel the romance bloom?"
Slow-dancing in the water's gloom!

A crab pens notes with tiny claws,
"Dear Lagoon, you're without flaws."
But a fish teased with bubbles near,
"Dear crab, your crush is quite unclear!"

At dusk, the moon starts to swoon,
With stars that twinkle, "What a tune!"
Letters float, unseen yet bright,
In love with this lagoon, what a night!

Chants of the Emerald Canopy

The parrots squawk, what a noise,
As monkeys swing and tease with poise.
A lizard slips, oh what a sight,
While bugs form bands, ready to bite.

The trees all sway with rhythmic grace,
Dancing leaves in a leafy race.
Squirrels giggle, toss their nuts,
While toucans jest with silly guts.

A sloth hangs low, thinks he's a star,
While ants march by, each one ajar.
"Is it lunchtime?" one ant inquires,
A buffet served, they toast with choirs.

Bananas sway from their lofty throne,
"They're ripe!" they shout, "Let's take a loan!"
So jungle life, with laughs so bold,
Is a cruise of fun, or so I'm told.

Vibrations of the Warmth

The sun beats down in radiant beams,
A coconut falls, or so it seems.
Tripping tourists, laughter erupts,
As waves come in, their boat erupts.

The parrots dance on sunlit days,
In pursuit of snacks, they've found new ways.
A crabs' ballet on golden sands,
While kids build castles, in funny bands.

A beach ball flies, with giggles ring,
It bounces back, like a rubber spring.
With sunscreen on, it's slip and slide,
One laughs so hard, he's swallowed pride.

Beneath the palms, a hammock sways,
As laughter floats in warm sun rays.
The tropics call, it's a lively scene,
Where joy and play make a perfect routine.

Moonlit Reflections on Still Waters

The moon peeks out, the waters glare,
Croaking frogs sing songs of despair.
"Is that a fish?" a frog will croak,
Then jumps right in, and, oh! He choked!

A firefly blinks, a little dance,
While turtles stroll, it's quite a chance.
A midnight snack, with bugs in tow,
With starlit skies that put on a show.

The wind whispers secrets, soft and sly,
"Did you hear that?" asks a nearby fly.
But he shushed himself, with a silly grin,
As moonbeams light the night to spin.

The water laps with rhythmic beats,
As fish flop up, and add to feats.
Each wave a laugh, a playful sound,
In moonlit bliss, fun can be found.

The Heartbeat of the Rainforest

In the heart of green, the wild things prance,
With every step, they take a chance.
An iguana stares, bold and spry,
While a snake slides by with a sly goodbye.

A toucan calls, with colors aflame,
"Hey, look at me!" it shrieks in fame.
A deer trots close, but then takes flight,
Comically missed with a funny fright.

Rain drips down from lofty heights,
The jungle laughs, in so many sights.
Frogs jump high, in splashy fun,
With puddles formed, they've just begun.

So listen close to the forest's song,
Where every laugh feels right, not wrong.
In tropical lands, with joy held dear,
The heartbeat thrums, let's give a cheer!

Melodic Rain on Tropical Leaves

Raindrops dance on leaves so green,
A slippery show, like a clown's routine.
Birds are laughing in a flurry,
Chasing tails, oh what a hurry!

Frogs in raincoats jump around,
Making music without a sound.
With each splash, a giggle shared,
This tropical rain, no one prepared!

Lizards slide on puddle paths,
Wearing tiny hats for laughs.
Palm trees sway, a funny sight,
Wishing upon a star so bright!

So here's to rain and leafy cheer,
With every drop, joy brings us near.
In this comedy of nature's play,
Let's laugh and dance throughout the day!

Swaying to Nature's Tempo

The breeze dips low, then sways up high,
Coconut shells all start to fly!
Monkeys join with monkey tunes,
While grasshoppers boogie under moons.

Laughter bounced on waves so bold,
As crabs danced cha-cha on the gold.
Turtles slow but still keep pace,
In this tropical, jolly race!

The cicadas buzz with silly rhymes,
While parrots improvise with times.
Coconuts fall, a "thud" then a cheer,
While fish make faces as they disappear!

So let's join in this merry beat,
Those who sway are never beat!
In this tropical fun, we thrive,
Grooving happily, we feel alive!

Jasmine Nights and Coconut Days

Under the stars, with jasmine's sweet,
I tripped on a coconut, oh what a feat!
Fireflies giggle, giving light,
As I stumble, laughter takes flight.

Daytime shines on sandy shores,
With mischief lurking, where laughter roars.
A crab in sunglasses struts by,
While the ocean waves tickle and sigh.

Seashells whisper the silliest tales,
Of wiggly fish and sailing snails.
Under the shade, we share our fun,
With coconut jokes, we're never done!

From jasmine nights to sunny ways,
Laughter lingers in every phrase.
So grab a shell, and join the cheer,
In this tropical world, joy is near!

Symphony of the Coral Reef

In the coral's swirl, fish dance along,
With fins like wings, they hum a song.
An octopus plays the bongo drum,
While anemones sway, and sea turtles strum.

Starfish spin in graceful stance,
As clown fish join the coral dance.
The sea is a stage, so we'll take a seat,
For this marine concert can't be beat!

The shrimps are chirping, they're quite a sight,
With tiny maracas, they shake with delight.
A sea turtle giggles, wearing a hat,
Dreaming of salsa with a wink and a chat.

So let's dive deep, join in the fun,
With fishy giggles under the sun.
In the symphony beneath the tide,
Tropical laughter we won't hide!

www.ingramcontent.com/pod-product-compliance
Lightning Source LLC
Chambersburg PA
CBHW072222070526
44585CB00015B/1445